LETTS POCKET GUIDE TO

TREES

Nearly 200 of the most common
European trees described and
illustrated in colour

Pamela Forey

CHARLES LETTS · *Letts* · FOUNDED 1796 ·

Conversion Table

1mm	= 0.039in	25cm	= 9.842in
5mm	= 0.196in	50cm	= 19.68in
1cm	= 0.394in	1m	= 39.37in
5cm	= 1.968in	5m	= 16.40ft
10cm	= 3.937in	10m	= 32.81ft

Front cover illustration: Beech Tree

This edition first published 1990
by Charles Letts & Co Ltd
Diary House, Borough Road,
London SE1 1DW

'Letts' is a registered trademark of
Charles Letts (Scotland) Ltd

This edition produced under licence by
Malcolm Saunders Publishing Ltd, London

© 1990 this edition Atlantis Publications Ltd

ISBN 1 85238 104 3

Printed in Spain

Contents

Introduction

The chief aim of this book is to enable the reader to identify positively and as simply as possible the great majority of European trees which he is likely to encounter.

A great number of people may not have the time or the opportunity to develop a detailed interest in trees but would appreciate some means by which they can easily identify a tree that may attract their attention, on holiday, for instance, or on a country walk, or simply one that catches the eye in a local park or garden.

Faced with tree books which contain the entire list of European trees, most people are quite bemused. Where do you start looking if, as is almost invariably the case, the trees are systematically grouped in families. The beginner, understandably, probably has little or no idea into which family a particular tree falls. So this book is arranged in a different way. The trees are grouped according to their leaf shapes, an easily recognizable feature.

The trees are all described and illustrated in their spring and autumn forms with autumn fruits, since it is at these times that the new observer is likely to be attracted by them. Emphasis is given to flowers and fruits, as well as to leaves, since, as well as being the most obvious, they are also the most characteristic and easily identifiable features of the tree.

Finally, this book does not claim to present a complete list with its 'featured trees' (those with an entire page including a full colour plate). In such a large area as Europe, there is wide variation in the species found from north to south. So trees that are rare or absent in the north may be common or even dominant in the south, and vice versa. A quick look at the special distribution box (see Fig. 2) will tell the reader whether he can expect to find that tree in his part of Europe. Some native trees have been omitted if they grow in remote areas where people seldom go or if they have limited distributions; other introduced or hybrid species have been included because they are commonly planted in streets or parks or gardens where the non-expert is likely to notice them and wonder what they are.

How to use this Book

This book is divided into three basic sections, *broad-leaved trees, palms and palm-like trees* and *conifers*. A fourth section, *lookalikes and cultivars*, complements the first three. These sections are clearly distinguished by the different coloured bands at the top of the page (see Fig. 1).

Fig. 1 Key to tree sections

▢	Broad-leaved trees	▢	Palms and palm-like trees
▢	Conifers	▢	Lookalikes and cultivars

Using the *Guide to Identification* to tree and leaf type overpage, first decide to which of the above sections your tree belongs. The leaf symbols will help you to narrow down the field and the information contained in the coloured boxes beneath the illustration of each tree make a positive identification possible and eliminate confusion. A specimen page is shown in Fig. 2.

PRIMARY FEATURES

Where feasible, the reader will be able to recognize the tree from the primary characteristics described in the first box, together with the illustration. However, sometimes it is a combination of features that identifies a tree, firstly as a type of tree (e.g. as an oak, if it has acorns) and then as a particular species (e.g. as a Common Oak if it has stalked acorns). The reader can be sure that he has identified the tree when it has all the characteristics of the first and second boxes.

However, trees present a time problem in that, for example, if the first box identifies the tree by its flowers, then this box can only be used at certain times of the year. The second box therefore includes complementary data on fruits and leaves which enable the reader to identify the tree at other times of the year.

FLOWERS AND FRUITS

You will also find flowering and fruiting times at the foot of the page, but it is important to realize that these are guides only. A tree growing in southern Europe will come into flower many weeks earlier than one of the same species growing in northern areas. Flowering times are probably more reliable guides on the whole than fruiting times, which tend to be much more variable. The fruiting times usually refer to ripe fruit – it is worth remembering

5

that if a tree flowers in spring or early summer and the fruiting time given is in the autumn, then the fruits will be visible throughout the summer, gradually growing and developing until they ripen. Therefore, fruits will often be present on a tree for much longer periods of time than the flowers and if allowance is made for immaturity of size and colour, then they can be used to help you in identification.

The third box is a general guide to the distribution of the trees in Europe (Britain is classified as being in northern or western Europe), and it also gives environmental details, including soil preferences, trees that grow in cities, beside water and so on.

AVOIDING CONFUSION

The fourth box on each page gives the names of similar trees with which the featured tree could be confused. All these 'lookalikes' are either featured in detail themselves or, if contained in brackets, appear under the heading of *Lookalikes and cultivars* in section 4.

The 'lookalikes' box is important for two reasons. Firstly, it is always possible to jump to conclusions when looking for known identifying features. You can in effect already have made up your mind on a tree's identity before checking out the primary points. Some species of trees resemble each other quite closely. Secondly, it is very important for the reader to become aware of exactly which groups of trees resemble each other so that he can check out the differences. This is where the guesswork ends and the skill begins.

Section 4 consists of 1) a group of less common species for which the featured trees may be mistaken; 2) a selection of common garden varieties of a few trees, including Japanese Cherries, Magnolias, Hollies and Eucalypts, all of which have so many varieties that they could not be given space enough in the featured trees sections; and 3) the commoner varieties of conifers, so popular as hedging and specimen trees in modern gardens.

CHECK YOUR SIGHTINGS

So now we come to it. This book is designed to fit into your pocket. Take it with you on your next walk! At last you can identify the tree on the corner where you sheltered from the rain, or the one in the next road that has such lovely blossom every year. But remember that trees grow very slowly, so treat the size indication with caution! Just because we have said that this is a large tree does not mean that you have identified it wrongly if it is small – it may be just young. But the leaves, flowers and fruits will not change for they are characteristic of that species of tree.

Now you know how to use this book. You are equipped with all the knowledge you need for the moment. Good luck – and don't forget to tick off your sightings on the check-list provided with the index.

Guide to Identification

BROAD-LEAVED TREES

Trees with a host of small, thin, broad leaves growing on woody branches which spread from one or several woody stems or trunks. These trees bear flowers at certain times of the year (some with petals like the Rowan or the Orange Tree; others with fluffy clusters of petal-less flowers like Ash or Elm; others with catkins like Willow or Oak) and most bear dry or juicy fruits. If your tree fits this description, then consult the following sub-sections:

Fig. 2 Specimen page

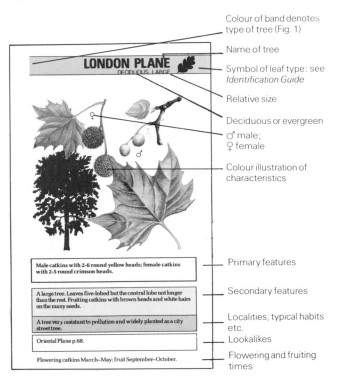

Colour of band denotes type of tree (Fig. 1)

Name of tree

LONDON PLANE
DECIDUOUS LARGE

Symbol of leaf type: see *Identification Guide*

Relative size

Deciduous or evergreen

♂ male; ♀ female

Colour illustration of characteristics

Male catkins with 2-6 round yellow heads; female catkins with 2-5 round crimson heads.

— Primary features

A large tree. Leaves five-lobed but the central lobe not longer than the rest. Fruiting catkins with brown heads and white hairs on the many seeds.

— Secondary features

A tree very resistant to pollution and widely planted as a city street tree.

— Localities, typical habits etc.

Oriental Plane p.68.

— Lookalikes

Flowering catkins March–May; fruit September–October.

— Flowering and fruiting times

Trees with simple leaves In these trees the leaves are entire and undivided and not lobed in any way. Very many trees have leaves of this type and so, to enable you to find your tree more quickly, we have divided the sub-section into three groups:

Simple leaves with single teeth In these trees the leaves have edges which may bear sharp or rounded, fine or coarse teeth. If the leaves of your tree are so finely toothed that you are unsure of their placement, or if some are toothed and some are not, then you should look in the section on trees with simple leaves without teeth as well.

This is quite a large group and the trees are arranged so that those having leaves with small teeth are at the beginning of the group and those having leaves with coarser teeth are at the end; a quick comparison will show you whether it would be better for you to start at the beginning of the group and work forwards or at the end and work backwards.

Simple leaves with double teeth In these trees the leaves have quite coarsely toothed edges in which the coarse teeth are also toothed – hence double teeth.

Simple leaves without teeth In these trees the edges of the leaves are generally toothless. However some of the leaves may have a few irregular teeth or the edges may be so finely toothed that it is really quite difficult to decide whether they are toothed or not. If in doubt, then you should check the beginning of the group of trees with simple leaves and single teeth as well. Some of the leaves in this group have edges that are wavy (see Beech p.51) or spiny or both. Spines are not the same as teeth (see Holly p.61, for example).

Trees with lobed leaves In these trees the blades of the leaves are divided into lobes, either pairs of lobes, as in the Common Oak diagram left, or into more triangular lobes, as in the Sycamore (p.75). In none of these leaves do the lobes extend to the base of the leaf or to the central line of the leaf, to divide it into separate leaflets. If you have a leaf which is split right to the base or to the central line, then you should look at the next section, on trees with compound leaves.

Trees with compound leaves The blades of these leaves are divided into either a few or many separate leaflets, usually along the length of the leaf as in the Rowan diagram left, but sometimes the leaflets all grow from one point at the top of the leafstalk as in the Horse Chestnut (p.85).

PALMS AND PALM-LIKE TREES

Trees in which the trunks are formed from old leaf-bases; they are not real, woody trunks at all. The leaves grow in a dense crown from the tops of the trunks and may be simple, fan-shaped or finely divided compound leaves. If your tree fits this description, then you can turn directly to the featured plants of this section.

CONIFERS

Trees with a regular appearance and very many small, either needle-like or scale-like leaves growing from woody branches spreading from a single woody trunk. These trees bear small separate male and female 'flowers' like miniature cones. The female flowers develop into mature cones which contain the seeds, or in a few species, into seed-bearing 'berries'. If your tree fits this description, then consult the following sub-sections:

Trees with needle-like leaves In these trees the leaves are like needles. They may grow in rows or spirals along the branches, or they may grow in clusters (see Cedar of Lebanon, p.104) or in pairs (see Scots Pine, p.108).

Trees with scale-like leaves In these trees the leaves are small and scale-like and clothe the branches so closely that the branches often look green and feathery. In a few trees the scale-like leaves are spiky as in the Chinese Juniper.

Further Reading

A Field Guide to the Trees of Britain and Northern Europe, Alan Mitchell. Collins, London, 1974.

Field Guide to the Trees and Shrubs of Britain, Readers Digest Nature Lover's Library, London, 1981.

The Oxford Book of Trees, A. R. Clapham and E. B. Nicholson. Oxford University Press, 1975.

Trees in Britain, Europe and North America, Roger Phillips, Pan, London, 1978.

Trees and Bushes of Britain and Europe, Oleg Polunin. Oxford University Press, 1976.

Trees and Shrubs hardy in the British Isles, W. J. Bean. John Murray, London, 1970.

Leaves glossy, dark green above, white below; only 2-4 times as long as broad, sticky and fragrant when young; growing on very shiny twigs.

A dense shrub or small tree. Catkins appearing after the leaves, more or less upright, male catkins yellow, female catkins green, later white and fluffy with seed; male and female catkins on separate trees.

Streamsides and other wet places.

Crack Willow p.14; Goat Willow p.49; (Almond Willow p.118).

Catkins May–June, seeding in June–July.

WHITE WILLOW

DECIDUOUS, MEDIUM

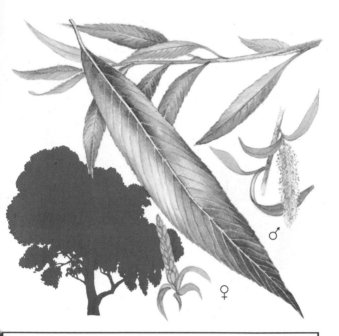

♂

♀

Leaves 5-10 times as long as broad, silky white above and below, on ascending branches.

A medium-sized tree, often pollarded. Catkins appearing with the leaves, male catkins yellow, female catkins green later white and fluffy when in seed, on separate trees.

Streamsides and other wet places.

Crack Willow p.14; (Almond Willow p.118).

Catkins April–May, seeding in June.

11

Characteristic long, weeping, yellow branches may touch the ground.

A large tree. Catkins usually male, sometimes with both male and female flowers on the same catkins. Leaves about 10 times as long as broad, green above, whitish below.

An introduced hybrid. Commonly planted throughout Europe especially beside water or in gardens.

(Chinese Weeping Willow p.118).

Catkins April–May; no fruit.

Young shoots very distinctive – dark purple, with whitish bloom. Leaves broadly oblong, only 2 – 4 times as long as broad and with crimson leaf-stalks.

A shrub or small tree. Catkins appearing before the leaves; almost stalkless, upright, male catkins yellow, female catkins grey-green later white and fluffy when in seed, on separate trees.

A northern European native, widely planted in wet places in more southern areas for its purple shoots.

Goat Willow p.49.

Catkins February–March, seeding in May–June.

♂

♀

Twigs breaking easily with an audible crack; leaves 4–9 times as long as broad, green above, paler beneath, on spreading, ascending branches.

A medium-sized tree, often pollarded. Catkins appearing with the leaves; drooping, male catkins yellow, female catkins green later white and fluffy when in seed, on separate trees.

Streamsides and other wet places.

White Willow p.11; (Almond Willow p.118).

Catkins April–May, seeding in June–July.

Flowers light rose-pink, single, solitary or in pairs, appearing before the leaves.

A small bushy tree bearing leathery, downy, green fruits. Seeds inside the fruit stones are the almonds.

Cultivated for its flowers in northern areas and for its nuts in southern areas of Europe.

(Peach p.118).

Flowers February–April; fruit May–July.

Flowers white, solitary, appearing before the leaves on short spine-tipped side branches – very striking against the blackish bark.

A dense, suckering shrub or small tree. Leaves dull green above, somewhat downy below, especially on the veins. Fruit is the sloe – small bluish-black acid berries with a definite bloom.

Forms dense thickets in hedgerows and woodland all over Europe except the extreme north.

Cherry Plum p.24.

Flowers March–April; fruit September–October.

Fruit is the plum – sweet, juicy fruits, 2–7.5cm long, yellow, red or purple in colour, drooping, in small clusters or solitary.

A small tree or suckering shrub. Flowers occur in clusters of 2 or 3, appearing with the leaves. Petals white, often have a greenish tinge, especially in bud. Leaves dull green above, almost smooth beneath.

Grown for its fruit and often naturalized in hedgerows all over Europe.

Cherry Plum p.24; (Copper Beech p.119).

Flowers March–May; fruit July–October.

Fruit is the pear – small, brownish in the wild tree, but garden escapes are common and these may have bigger, more yellow fruit.

A medium-sized tree with ascending branches. Clusters of about 5 white flowers appear before the leaves are fully open; naturalized trees may have mistletoe growing on them.

Hedgerows or orchards. Cultivated forms are grown in gardens and orchards.

Apple p.23.

Flowers April–May; fruit July–October.

Flowers white, bell-shaped, fragrant, in long drooping chains.

A medium-sized tree with greyish-brown, peeling bark which has a strong foetid smell. Fruits are blue-black, bitter cherries, each about 8mm in length, in drooping chains.

Found in most European countries especially on lime-rich soils. Planted in streets and gardens.

(Rum Cherry p.118).

Flowers May; fruit July–September.

PORTUGUESE LAUREL
EVERGREEN, SMALL

Distinctive red leaf-stalks on long, leathery, dark green leaves.

A dense, domed shrub or small tree. Flowers small, fragrant, creamy white in many-flowered spikes; fruit very small, brownish berries, in long chains.

Native to parts of southern Europe and widely planted, especially as a hedge, further north.

Cherry Laurel p.56; Sweet Bay p.57.

Flowers June; fruit August–October.

Fruits are deep pink, 4-lobed capsules, opening to expose seeds in bright orange seed covers.

A shrub or small tree with many branches. Leaves opposite, lance-shaped. Flowers greenish-yellow in small clusters in axils of leaves.

Woods, hedgerows and scrub, especially on lime-rich soils, over much of Europe except the north and south.

Japanese Spindle Tree p.118.

Flowers May–June; fruit September–October.

21

Fruits are round, purple-black berries with yellow pips, occurring singly or in small clusters.

A shrub or small tree. Twigs bear opposite leaves and end in thorns. Flowers are sweetly scented, small, greenish, in small clusters at the bases of the young shoots; male and female flowers on separate trees.

Hedges and scrub over much of Europe except the Mediterranean region.

Alder Buckthorn p.50.

Flowers May–June; fruit August–September.

Fruit is small, reddish-yellow apple, sour and hard.

A small tree. Flowers form in clusters of 3-4, white, suffused with pink, appearing with the leaves on short side branches. Occasionally may have mistletoe growing on it.

Hedgerows, scrub, woodland, over much of Europe. Naturalized cultivated apples have larger, sweeter fruit.

Pear p.18.

Flowers May; fruit September–October.

Fruit smooth, round, sweet, red or yellow, 2–3.5cm long, growing singly, but not always produced in more northern areas.

A shrub or small round-headed tree. White flowers are solitary or in clusters of 2-3, appearing with the leaves; usually the first cherry to flower. A purple-leaved form with pink flowers is commonly planted.

Commonly planted in streets and gardens, also cultivated for its fruit.

Blackthorn p.16; Plum p.17.

Flowers March; fruit July–September.

Flowers creamy-white, tubular, in large, flat clusters on the ends of shoots.

A shrub or small tree. Leaves rounded, opposite, wrinkled, felted on both surfaces but felting persisting only on lower surface. Fruit a flat cluster of many oval berries, red at first later black.

Hedges, thickets, edges of woods throughout much of Europe except extreme north.

None.

Flowers May–June; fruit September onwards.

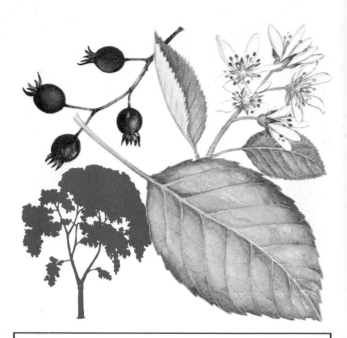

Very distinctive appearance in spring, when opening buds have a whitish appearance because of the white under-surfaces of the young leaves and the white flower buds.

A shrub or small tree. White star-like flowers occur in small upright clusters in the axils of the leaves. Fruits are small berries, red at first, later blue-black, often occurring singly.

Open woodland, limestone uplands, over much of Europe. Often planted in parks and gardens.

Several other very similar species of mespils are grown in Europe.

Flowers April–May; fruit July–August.

Clusters of 2-6 small cherries, at first yellow flushed with red then dark purple-red unless eaten by birds first.

A medium-sized tree with many suckers, and reddish-brown bark. Flowers white in dense clusters, appearing just before the leaves.

Found over much of Europe except extreme north and south; a double-flowered variety is often planted in gardens.

Japanese Cherries p.28, 123 (Sour Cherry p.118).

Flowers April–May; fruit June.

Variety illustrated is 'Kanzan'

Flowers large, bright pink (white or light pink in some varieties), double or semi-double, in clusters, usually opening just before the leaves.

A large group of medium-sized trees often with spreading or even horizontal branches. Many have bronze-coloured young leaves. They are usually sterile.

Introduced and cultivated varieties widely planted in streets and gardens throughout Europe.

Many different varieties, see page 123. Gean p.27.

Flowers April–May; no fruit.

LOMBARDY POPLAR

DECIDUOUS, MEDIUM

♂

Branches all ascending to give a very characteristic narrow outline to this medium-sized tree.

Trees almost all male; male catkins reddish, not fluffy. Leaves often triangular in outline, leaf-stalks yellow-green in colour, flattened.

Frequently planted as windbreaks over much of Europe especially in lowland areas.

(Black Poplar p.118; Black Italian Poplar p.118).

Flowers March–April; no fruit.

DOWNY BIRCH
DECIDUOUS, SMALL/MEDIUM

Female flowering catkins grey-green; male catkins bright yellow; seeds numerous, winged, not fluffy, in greenish-brown fruiting catkins.

A small or medium-sized tree with one or several trunks. Bark greyish-white with brown horizontal bands. Male and female catkins on same tree. Young twigs and leaf-stalks covered with soft down, leaves often diamond-shaped.

Northern Europe and southern European mountain areas on poor acid soils.

Silver Birch p.42.

Catkins April–May, seeding in July–August.

Characteristic flying bracts at first bear small clusters of
yellowish-white flowers, later clusters of small ribless,
thin-shelled nutlets, both on the upper side.

A large tree, often with bosses on its otherwise smooth trunk –
areas of twigs and short shoots. Leaves 3–6cm long, heart-
shaped with pointed tips.

Grows wild throughout much of Europe except extreme north;
also planted as a street tree.

Large-leaved Lime p.32; Common Lime p.33.

Flowers July; fruit August–September.

31

Characteristic flying bracts at first bear small clusters of
yellowish-white flowers, later clusters of small heavily
ribbed, woody nutlets, both from the lower side.

A large tree with a smooth, grey trunk, bosses very rare. Leaves
6–12cm long, heart-shaped with pointed tips.

Native to central and southern Europe; extensively planted as a
street tree in more northern areas.

Small-leaved Lime p.31; Common Lime p.33.

Flowers June; fruit July–September.

COMMON LIME
DECIDUOUS, LARGE

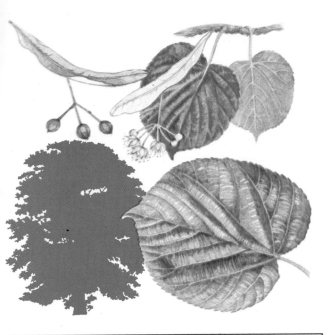

Characteristic flying bracts at first bear small clusters of
yellowish-white flowers, later clusters of small slightly
ribbed, woody nutlets, both from its lower side.

A large tree in which the trunk is covered with bosses – large
areas of twigs and shoots. Leaves 6–10cm long, heart-shaped
with pointed tips, often infested with aphids which drip
honeydew on to the ground beneath.

Often occurs in the wild as a hybrid of the other two limes.
Frequently planted as a street tree.

Small-leaved Lime p.31; Large-leaved Lime p.32.

Flowers July: fruit August-September.

Fruit a dense cylindrical cluster of many berries, 2–2.5cm long, at first green, ripening to deep red, berries very acid until ripe.

A low, domed tree with large rough, sometimes almost lobed leaves. Young shoots with milky juice. Male and female flowers pale green, in separate spikes, both very small and on same tree.

Cultivated for its fruit in much of Europe; occasionally naturalized.

(White Mulberry p.119).

Flowers May: fruit July-September.

Flowers white, bell-shaped in hanging clusters appearing in autumn, together with the ripening berries from the previous year.

A wide-topped small to medium-sized tree with brown fibrous bark and leathery, dark green leaves. Berries are rounded and warty, yellow at first ripening to deep red.

Thickets and the edges of woodland, especially on hillsides in southern and western Europe.

(Eastern Strawberry Tree p.119).

Flowers and fruit October–December.

Male catkins fluffy and brown with yellow pollen; female catkins purple at first, later white and fluffy with seed; the two kinds of catkin are on separate trees.

A medium-sized tree with many suckers. Often called Trembling Aspen from the constant shivering of the leaves – this caused by the very flattened, whitish leaf-stalks.

Forms thickets on poor, damp soils especially in northern and mountain areas.

Grey Poplar p.40: (Black Poplar p.118).

Catkins February–March, seeding in May.

Characteristic nettle-shaped leaves have long, twisted tips. Small, yellow, solitary flowers grow on long stalks in the axils of the leaves in late spring.

A medium-sized, round-headed tree. Fruits are small, solitary, brown berries, growing on long stalks in the axils of the leaves.

Native to southern Europe where it is often planted as a street tree.

None.

Flowers May; fruit September.

WHITEBEAM

DECIDUOUS, MEDIUM

Young shoots, leaves and flower stalks all covered in dense white wool; leaves retaining a white woolly underside all summer.

A medium-sized tree or large shrub. Flowers white in large, flat clusters; fruit bright red berries in similar clusters. Leaves very variable in shape, some almost lobed or with very deep teeth.

Grows throughout much of Europe especially on chalk; often planted as a street tree.

Swedish Whitebeam p.78; Wild Service Tree p.79.

Flowers May–June; fruit September–October.

SWEET CHESTNUT

♂

♀

Spiny green cups split open to reveal several deep brown shining nuts.

A large tree with wide spreading branches. Leaves large, up to 25cm long. Flowers in bisexual catkins, a few green female flowers at the base, yellow male flowers along most of the length of the catkins.

Cultivated and naturalized over most of Europe.

None.

Flowers July; fruit October.

GREY POPLAR
DECIDUOUS, LARGE

Male catkins reddish with grey fur and yellow pollen; female catkins rare; the two kinds of catkin on separate trees.

A large spreading tree with many suckers. Young leaves grey-downy, the down not persisting. Summer leaves on the suckers simple, not lobed, but with deep teeth. Female catkins when present, green, later white and fluffy with seed.

Wet woodland in much of Europe; mostly spreading by means of suckers.

White Poplar p.73; Aspen p.36.

Catkins February–March, seeding in April.

♀ ♀ ♂

Fruiting catkins are dark brown and stalked, like small
cones, and remain on the tree after the winged seeds have
gone until the following year.

A medium-sized tree. Leaves almost round. Male catkins in
small clusters, purple in winter, yellow in spring; female
catkins purple, becoming green in fruit, then brown and
woody.

Beside water and in fens throughout most of Europe.

(Green Alder p.119; Grey Alder p. 119).

Catkins February–April, fruiting catkins persistent.

41

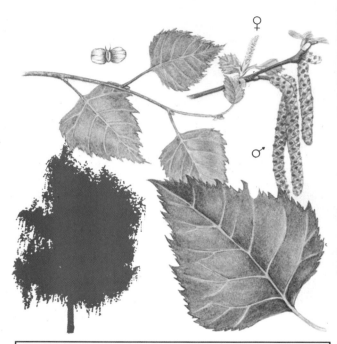

Bark smooth, silvery white and peeling with black diamond-shaped markings. Smaller branches drooping.

A medium-sized tree. Male catkins in clusters, brownish in winter, yellow with pollen in spring; female catkins grey-green in winter, brownish-green in spring, both on the same tree. Seeds with two wings, numerous.

Grows on acid soils over much of Europe.

Downy Birch p.30.

Catkins April–May, seeding in July–August.

HAZEL OR COBNUT
DECIChUOUS, SMALL

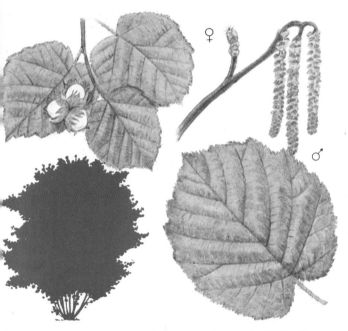

♀
♂

Male catkins long and yellow in drooping clusters; female flowers tiny red spikes appearing just after the male catkins of the same plant have shed their pollen.

A shrub or small tree with ascending branches. Leaves almost round. Fruits grow in green cups with ragged edges.

Hedgerows, woodlands and in gardens throughout Europe.

(Filbert p.120).

Flowers January–April; fruit September–October.

Leaves 8-16cm long, very rough, with one side having an ear-like projection at the base which covers the very short leaf-stalk.

A large domed tree with no suckers. Flowers dark purple clusters; fruits round and winged with a central seed, numerous.

Woods and hedgerows throughout much of Europe before Dutch Elm Disease destroyed the trees of whole areas.

English Elm p.45; Smooth Elm p.46; (Dutch Elm p.119)

Flowers February–March; fruit May–July.

Leaves 4.5–9cm long and rough; ear-like projection at the base of one side of the leaf which does not cover the leaf-stalk.

A large tree with a narrow crown and many suckers and twigs growing from the trunk. Many clusters of dark red flowers are borne, however fruits are not always formed or are often sterile.

Very characteristic of hedgerows before Dutch Elm Disease wiped out whole areas of trees.

Wych Elm p.44; Smooth Elm p.46 (Dutch Elm p.119).

Flowers February–March; fruits May–June (if produced).

45

Leaves 2.5–11.5cm long and smooth. Ear-like projection at base of one side of the leaf does not cover the leaf-stalk or may not be present at all.

A large tree with a narrow crown and many suckers and twigs growing from the trunk. Flowers are red clusters but fruit is rarely produced.

Native to much of Europe and often planted as a street tree before Dutch Elm Disease.

Wych Elm p.44; English Elm p.45; (Dutch Elm p.119).

Flowers February–March; Fruit April–May (if produced).

Fruiting spike consists of about 8 pairs of small nuts, each one cupped in a three-lobed bract, at first green later brown, the whole making a loose bunch.

A medium-sized tree in which the twigs grow horizontally in a zig-zag pattern. Male catkins up to 5cm long, greenish-yellow, drooping. Female catkins about 2cm long, green, drooping.

Hedgerows, woods, sometimes coppiced; sometimes planted as a street tree. Over much of Europe.

Hop Hornbeam p.48; Beech p.51.

Flowers April–May; fruit July–October.

47

Fruiting spike consists of about 15 small nuts, each one enclosed in a bladder, at first green later whitish, the whole forming a tight bunch.

A medium-sized tree, sometimes with several trunks. The male catkins are up to 10cm long, yellow and drooping. The female catkins are small, green, amongst the emerging leaves.

Woodlands and well-drained slopes in southern Europe; occasionally introduced further north.

Hornbeam p.47.

Flowers April; fruit September–October.

48

GOAT WILLOW
DECIDUOUS, SMALL

♂   ♀

Male catkins conspicuous on bare branches, upright, stalkless, silvery at first, yellow with pollen later.

A shrub or small tree. Female catkins upright, stalkless, green at first, appearing before the leaves, later white and fluffy with seed. Male and female catkins on separate trees.

Woodlands, hedgerows and scrub over much of Britain and continental Europe.

(Grey Willow p.118); Violet Willow p.13.

Catkins March–April, seeding in May.

Round berries, solitary or in pairs, grow on stalks from the axils of leaves, yellow at first, later red, then black.

A shrub or small tree. Twigs thornless with alternate leaves. Flowers small, white-green, solitary or in pairs in the axils of the leaves.

Moist heathland and fens, damp open woodland throughout much of Europe except the extreme north and south.

Buckthorn p.22.

Flowers May–June; fruit July–November.

Spiky brown cupules split into four lobes to reveal shiny brown three-angled nuts – the beech nuts.

A large tree. Leaves oval with pointed tips and wavy margins, very bright distinctive green when young. Male flowers pale yellow clusters, female flowers in pairs, green, both appearing with the leaves on the same tree.

Beechwoods are common on well-drained soils throughout Europe particularly on chalk.

Hornbeam p.47; (Copper Beech p.119).

Flowers May; fruit September–October.

51

Fruit an acorn. Leaves entire with wavy margins and occasional spines; dark green above and grey-furry below.

A large tree with a dense evergreen crown. Male catkins long and drooping, pale green, later gold with pollen; female flowers small, greenish-grey and furry.

Native to the Mediterranean region and widely grown in more northern areas of Europe.

Cork Oak p.53; (Kermes Oak p.120).

Flowers June, acorns ripen in October.

Fruit an acorn. Leaves entire with wavy, spiny margins, dark green above, grey and furry below.

A medium-sized tree with a heavy, dense crown. Bark is thick with commercial cork, which is stripped off leaving bare red wood. Male catkins green, in clusters; female flowers small, in axils of new leaves.

Dry hills of the Mediterranean region; widely planted for its cork.

Holm Oak p.52; (Kermes Oak p.120).

Flowers April–May, acorns ripen in October.

53

Fruit brown and oval like a rose-hip, at first hard, later becoming soft and edible – the medlar.

Wild form a crooked, thorny shrub; cultivated form a thornless tree. Young twigs, leaves and flower stalks covered with fine white down. Flowers large, solitary, with five white petals.

Wild form grows in hedgerows and woodlands in much of Europe except the north, cultivated form in gardens.

None.

Flowers May–June; fruit September–November.

54

Fruit hard; pear-shaped or round; yellow, sweet-smelling when ripe – the quince.

A small tree. Young twigs and undersides of leaves white and woolly. Flowers solitary, pink, bowl-shaped, borne in the axils of the leaves.

Hedgerows and copses and grown in gardens for its fruit in much of Britain and continental Europe, especially the southern areas.

(Japonica p.118).

Flowers May; fruit September–October.

Large, leathery, evergreen leaves have pale green leaf-stalks; flowers in an upright spike, creamy white.

A spreading shrub or small tree, often wider than tall. Fruit small, black, juicy berries in a chain. All parts of the plant are poisonous.

Widely planted in parks and gardens in much of Britain and continental Europe and often naturalized.

Portuguese Laurel p.20; Sweet Bay p.57; (Rhododendron p.119).

Flowers April; fruit August–September.

Dark green, leathery, evergreen leaves have dark red
leaf-stalks and an aromatic scent when crushed – widely
used in cooking.

A dense shrub or small tree. Flowers small, pale yellow, in pairs
in the axils of the leaves. Fruits are green berries, later turning
black.

A native of the Mediterranean and often planted for ornament
there and further north; not hardy.

Portuguese Laurel p.20; Cherry Laurel p.56.

Flowers March–April; fruit August–October.

LILAC
DECIDUOUS, SMALL

Characteristic flowers in large cones, pink, white or purple, fragrant; each flower is tubular in shape.

A shrub or small tree with many suckers. Leaves opposite, hairless, yellow-green, large and rounded. Fruit a cluster of brown capsules.

Scrub in Balkans; widely cultivated in gardens and parks; sometimes naturalized in hedgerows.

None.

Flowers May–June; fruit September.

Variety illustrated is Magnolia x soulangeana

Flowers large, cup-shaped, solitary, with a multitude of white or pink petals, borne at the tips of the shoots.

Mostly low-growing, spreading trees but some medium-sized species and some species evergreen. Leaves large and dark green above, often furry below.

A large group of introduced trees widely planted for ornament.

(About 35 species of magnolias, see page 123. Tulip Tree p.120).

Flowers in spring, summer or autumn depending on species.

59

Branches clothed in very small, opposite, dark green, glossy leaves with pale orange, hairy leaf-stalks.

A shrub or small tree. Flowers small, greenish-yellow in clusters in axils of leaves. Fruits small, greyish, rounded capsules.

Cultivated varieties used in hedges in much of Europe except extreme north; a native of southern hillsides.

None.

Flowers March–April; fruit August–September.

HOLLY
EVERGREEN, SMALL

Fruits are red berries in clusters in the axils of the leaves in mid-winter.

A shrub or small tree. Leaves with prickly edges, dark green and glossy above, paler beneath. Flowers white, fragrant, in clusters in axils of the leaves.

In beech or oak woodland in much of Europe and often cultivated in shelter belts or as a hedge.

(There are many cultivated varieties of holly with different colours and spines on the leaves, see page 124.)

Flowers May–June; fruit November–December.

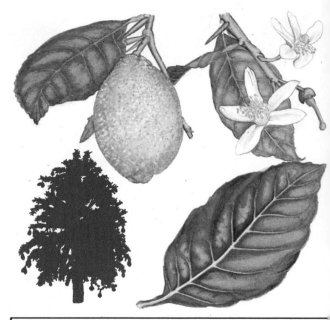

Fruit oval, pale yellow, with a distinctive scent and sour flesh – the lemon.

A small tree. Leaves thin and leathery, sometimes with irregular teeth; leaf-stalks are narrowly winged. Twigs bear pointed, green thorns. Flowers white, flushed with red, solitary and sweetly scented.

Cultivated throughout the Mediterranean region.

(Citron p.119).

Flowers in spring; fruit end autumn (native climes).

Fruit rounded, orange-yellow, with a distinctive scent and sweet flesh.

A small tree. Leaves thin and leathery, with wavy margins and narrowly winged leaf-stalks. Twigs not thorny. Flowers white, solitary and sweetly scented.

Cultivated for its fruit throughout the Mediterranean region.

(Seville Orange p.119).

Flowers in spring; fruit end autumn and winter (native climes).

Flowers bright pink, pea-like, in clusters, appearing before the leaves, growing directly out of larger branches as well as from smaller twigs.

A small tree. Leaves almost round or kidney-shaped. Fruits like pea-pods, dark red or brown, in clusters.

Dry rocky areas in the Mediterranean region. Introduced into gardens and parks in more northern areas.

None.

Flowers March–May; fruit July–September.

Fruits are edible, succulent and oily, green at first, turning black over the course of the following year.

A small gnarled tree. Leaves opposite. Flowers white, fragrant, in chains in the axils of the leaves.

Open woodland and thickets on rocky hillsides in the Mediterranean region; grown for its fruits.

None.

Flowers July–August; fruit September–October.

Variety illustrated is Tasmanian Blue Gum

Two kinds of leaves on the same tree – juvenile leaves, often blue and clasping the stem, sometimes green with short stalks; adult leaves long, drooping, lance-shaped.

Medium-sized or large trees, often graceful. Flowers fluffy white clusters in the axils of the leaves. Flower buds form on the tree up to a year before they open.

Widely grown in parks and gardens and also commercially for their oil, timber and for paper.

A large group of trees native to Australia of which about 12 are commonly grown in Europe, see page 124.

Flowers open in late summer.

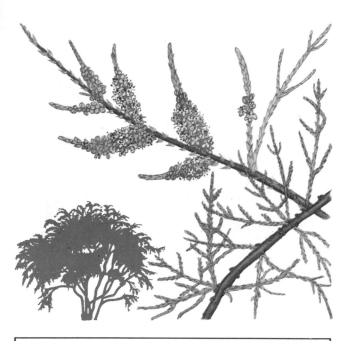

Leaves very small, scale-like, sheathing the twigs, giving the plant a feathery appearance.

A shrub or small tree with very slender, graceful branches. Flowers pink or white in many dense clusters along the branches.

Often near the sea in southern Europe; planted and naturalized further north.

None.

Flowers April–September; fruit July–October.

ORIENTAL PLANE
DECIDUOUS, LARGE

Male catkins with 2–7 round, yellow heads; female catkins
with 2–6 round, flattened heads, dark red when in full bloom.

A large tree. Leaves five-lobed with the central lobe much longer
than the others. Fruiting catkins with brownish-green heads and
fine hooked spines on the seeds.

Widely planted in parks and gardens especially in southern
Europe.

London Plane p.69.

Flowering catkins April–June; fruit September–October.

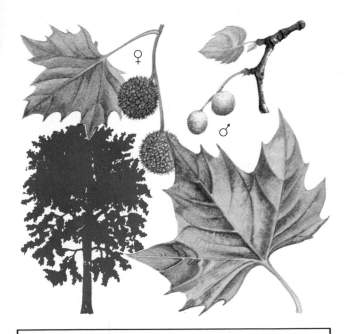

Male catkins with 2-6 round yellow heads; female catkins
with 2-5 round crimson heads.

A large tree. Leaves five-lobed but the central lobe not longer
than the rest. Fruiting catkins with brown heads and white hairs
on the many seeds.

A tree very resistant to pollution and widely planted as a city
street tree.

Oriental Plane p.68.

Flowering catkins March–May; fruit September–October.

♂

Fruits are acorns. Acorn cups relatively smooth, growing on stalks between 2–8cm long, looking like a miniature smoker's pipe.

A large broad tree. Leaves with 3-6 pairs of wavy-edged lobes and with small ear-like projections at the base. Male catkins yellow, in clusters, very slender. Female flowers terminal on new shoots, brownish, tiny.

Woodlands, hedgerows, mainly on heavy lime-rich soils throughout much of Europe except extreme north and south.

Sessile Oak p.71; Turkey Oak p.72.

Flowers April–May; acorns ripen in September–October.

70

SESSILE OR DURMAST OAK

DECIDUOUS, LARGE

♂

Fruits are acorns. Acorn cups relatively smooth, with a very short stalk of less than 1cm or stalkless.

A large, domed tree. Leaves with 4–6 pairs of wavy-edged lobes and without small ear-like projections at the base. Male catkins greenish-yellow, in clusters, very slender. Female flowers tiny, whitish, in leaf axils.

Woodlands, hedgerows, mainly on acid, sandy soils throughout much of Europe except extreme north and south.

Common Oak p.70; Turkey Oak p.72.

Flowers April–May; acorns ripen in September–October.

Fruits are acorns. Acorn cups are stalkless, covered with long, curly, spreading scales.

A large, domed tree with variable leaves. Leaves with 7–8 pairs of blunt lobes but without ear-like projections at the base. Male catkins red, in dense clusters, later brown. Female flowers tiny, yellow, in leaf axils.

Planted as a roadside and parkland tree in much of Europe. Native to the woodlands of southern Europe.

Common Oak p.70; Sessile Oak p.71.

Flowers April–June; acorns ripen in September.

Male catkins red and grey-fluffy; female catkins green at first, later fluffy with seed.

A large spreading tree with many suckers. Young shoots and undersides of leaves with bright, white, furry down. Summer leaves of suckers always lobed, other leaves very variable in shape, basically rounded.

In wet woodland and on coasts, often spreading by suckers. Widely planted in much of Europe in gardens and streets.

Grey Poplar p.40.

Catkins March–April, seeding in June.

73

Characteristic fruits in winged pairs have wings curving away from each other.

A large spreading tree. Flowers greenish-yellow in large, broad, upright clusters of 30–40 flowers. Leaves large, with 5–7 pointed, toothed lobes; leaf-stalks red with milky juice.

Woodlands, hedgerows in much of Europe but only in uplands in southern Europe; an occasional street tree.

Sycamore p.75; (Japanese Maple p.120).

Flowers March–April; fruit September–October.

Characteristic fruits in winged pairs have wings curving towards each other.

A large, spreading tree. Flowers yellow-green in large, drooping, narrow clusters of 60–100 flowers. Leaves with 5, pointed, toothed lobes; leaf-stalks red without milky juice.

Woodlands, hedgerows in much of Europe; extensively introduced and naturalized; a common street tree.

Norway Maple p.74; (Japanese Maple p.120).

Flowers April–June; fruit September–October.

FIELD MAPLE

Characteristic fruits in winged pairs with wings spreading horizontally, often tinged with red.

A shrub or small tree. Flowers pale green in small, upright clusters of 10–20 flowers. Leaves small, with 3–5 rounded lobes; leaf-stalks red with milky juice.

Hedgerows, woodland and scrub on lime-rich soils especially in northern areas of Europe.

(Montpelier Maple p.120.)

Flowers April–May; fruit September–October.

Fruits are large clusters of round, deep red, single-stoned berries developing from similar clusters of white, pink-tinged, heavily scented flowers.

A large, dense, thorny shrub or small tree. Leaves with 3–7 deep rounded lobes, green and mostly hairless on both surfaces.

Very common in woodland, hedgerows and scrubland throughout Europe.

(Midland Hawthorn p.120.)

Flowers March–June; fruit August–November.

Fruits are large clusters of oblong, red-brown berries developing from similar clusters of white flowers in which the flower-stalks are covered with grey down.

A shrub or small tree. Leaves longer than broad with 6–8 pairs of small lobes, grey-woolly beneath, especially when young.

A northern European species, often planted as a street tree in more southern areas.

Whitebeam p.38; Wild Service Tree p.79.

Flowers May; fruit September.

Fruits are clusters of long, brown berries developing from similar clusters of white flowers in which the flower-stalks are woolly.

A medium-sized, spreading tree. Leaves broader than long, with 3–4 pairs of triangular, toothed lobes, green on both sides, somewhat woolly below.

Woodlands, scattered throughout much of Europe.

(Service Tree of Fontainebleau p.120); Norway Maple p.74; Sycamore p.75.

Flowers May–June; fruit September.

Fruits large, succulent, pear-shaped, solitary and green.

A shrub or small tree, often trained against a wall. Twigs with milky juice. Leaves dark green, leathery or rough, with 3–7 deep, rounded lobes. Male and female flowers in separate flask-shaped receptacles.

Cultivated for its fruit throughout southern Europe; also grows in more northern areas.

None.

Flowers June–September; fruit July–October.

80

TREE OF HEAVEN
DECIDUOUS, MEDIUM

Large, hanging clusters of winged fruits, usually brown, sometimes reddish, each with a seed at the centre of the twisted wing.

A medium-sized tree. Leaves up to 1 metre long with 13–41 leaflets, each one with a red stalk and 2–4 teeth near the base. Flowers unpleasantly scented, greenish, in large clusters at the ends of the shoots.

Grown as a street tree and in parks throughout Europe.

None.

Flowers July–August; fruit August–September.

COMMON ASH
DECIDUOUS, MEDIUM

Large, hanging clusters of winged fruits, at first green later brown; each 2–5.5cm long with a seed at the base of the wing.

A medium-sized tree. Leaves opposite, up to 30cm long with 7–13 leaflets. Flowers petalless, purple clusters appearing before the leaves which open in early summer.

Woodland especially on lime-rich soils, throughout Europe.

Manna Ash p.83; (Narrow-leaved Ash p.120).

Flowers April–May; fruit October–November.

Large, hanging clusters of winged fruits, at first green, later brown, each 1.5-2.5cm long with a seed at the base of the wing.

A small tree. Leaves opposite, up to 30cm long, with 5–9 leaflets. Flowers with creamy white, scented petals appearing with the leaves in pyramidal clusters.

Native to the Mediterranean region in woods and thickets; also planted in parks and gardens in more northern areas.

Common Ash p.82; (Narrow–leaved Ash p.120).

Flowers April–May; fruit July–September.

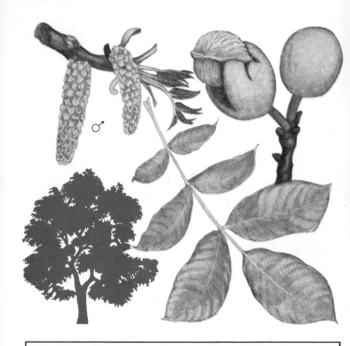

Round, smooth, green fruits enclose the wrinkled stones.
The seeds are edible nuts.

A large spreading tree. Leaves up to 45cm long, with 3–9
(usually 7) leaflets; basal leaflets smaller than terminal ones.
Male catkins yellow, drooping; female flowers small, green; both
on young shoots.

Planted and naturalized throughout much of Europe.

None.

Flowers May–June; fruit September–October.

84

Round, green, softly spiny fruits enclose 1–3 brown, shiny
seeds – the horse chestnuts or 'conkers'.

A large spreading tree. Leaves with 5–7 leaflets, all growing
from the same point and with long leaf-stalks. Flowers white or
pink in large, showy pyramidal clusters.

Extensively planted and naturalized in towns and cities
throughout much of Europe; a common street tree.

(Red Horse Chestnut p.120.)

Flowers April–May; fruit September.

SERVICE TREE
DECIDUOUS, MEDIUM

Fruit a small cluster of green or brown pear-shaped berries with gritty flesh.

A medium-sized tree with a domed crown. Leaves with 13–21 toothed leaflets, up to 22cm long. Flowers with five separate, creamy white petals, in large clusters; flower-stalks downy.

Planted as an ornamental tree and naturalized throughout much of Europe; also grown for its fruit.

Rowan p.87.

Flowers May; fruit July–August.

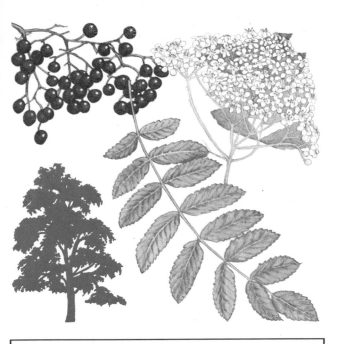

Large clusters of berries, at first yellow turning orange then quickly red to be devoured by the birds.

A small or medium-sized tree. Leaves with 9–19 toothed leaflets, up to 25cm long. Flowers with 5 separate, creamy white petals and downy flower-stalks, in large clusters.

Hedgerows and hillsides over much of Europe; often planted as a street tree.

Service Tree p.86.

Flowers May; fruit July (yellow) – September (red).

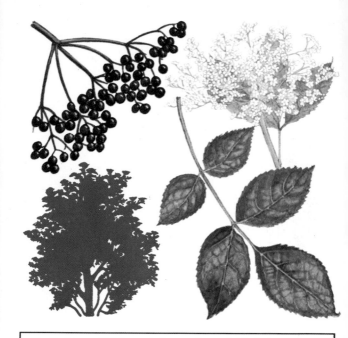

Fruit a heavy, flat-topped cluster of round, black, juicy berries.

A shrub or small tree often with arching branches. Leaves opposite, with 3–9 toothed leaflets. Flowers white, scented, tubular, in large flat-topped clusters; flower-stalks not downy.

Damp woodland, waste places and hedgerows throughout much of Europe.

None.

Flowers June–July; fruits August–November.

Flowers bright yellow, pea-like, in long, loose, drooping chains.

A small tree. Leaves with 3 leaflets. Fruits like pea-pods, green and hairy when young, dry and brown when mature; up to 10 black seeds in each pod. The whole plant is very poisonous.

Woods and scrub in southern Europe. Widely planted in streets and gardens throughout much of Europe.

(Scotch Laburnum p.120.)

Flowers May–June; fruit July–August.

89

Flowers white, sweet-scented, like sweet peas in drooping clusters.

A medium-sized tree, often with many suckers. Leaves up to 20cm long with 13–15 leaflets, yellowish in colour and often with a spine at the base. Fruits are like clusters of brown pea-pods.

Hedgerows, parks and gardens especially in western and southern Europe on sandy soils.

None.

Flowers June; fruit October.

90

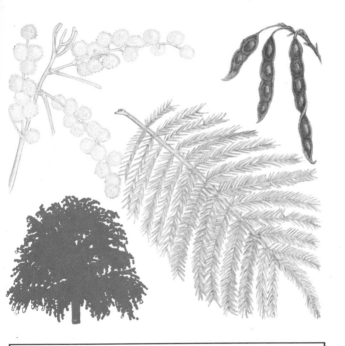

Flowers bright yellow, fragrant balls in long, drooping chains.

A medium-sized tree. Leaves up to 12cm long with 13–25 pairs of feathery leaflets, silvery grey or yellowish green in colour. Fruits are like flattened pea-pods.

Introduced and widely planted in southern Europe for ornament and to stabilize sandy soils and dunes.

None.

Flowers January–February; fruits May.

Leaves lance-shaped, up to 90cm long, sharp-pointed, dark green and fibrous.

A palm-like tree with several 'trunks' and suckers, each with a dense crown of leaves. Flowers creamy white and fragrant, in large spikes over 1 metre tall. Fruits are bluish-white berries.

Streets, parks and gardens in coastal areas of southern and western Europe.

None.

Flowers in spring (native climes).

Leaves up to 1 metre in diameter, fan-shaped, divided into 50–60 stiff, pointed lobes and with leaf-stalks covered with long, brown fibres.

A medium-sized tree with a crown of leaves growing from the top of the trunk and with dead leaves partly covering the trunk. Flowers yellow, fragrant, growing in a large spike. Fruits like purple berries.

The most hardy and most widely planted of all the palms; only flowering in more southern areas.

Dwarf Fan Palm p.94.

Flowers and fruits; continuous in tropical climate.

☀ DWARF FAN PALM
EVERGREEN, SMALL

Leaves up to 1 metre in diameter, fan-shaped, divided into 12–20 stiff, lance-shaped leaflets. Leaf-stalks armed with sharp spines.

A dwarf palm with a short trunk and many suckers, forming a dense clump. Flowers yellow, often hidden, in large dense clusters. Fruits brown inedible berries.

The only native European palm, growing on sandy coastlines in the western Mediterranean.

Chusan Palm p.93.

Flowers and fruits; continuous in tropical climate.

Leaves 5–6 metres long, compound, with 100–200 pairs of spiny leaflets in a dense crown of up to 200 leaves at the top of stout 'trunk'.

A medium-sized tree. Flowers in large clusters in the axils of the leaves developing into large clusters of smooth, brown fruits with dry, tasteless flesh.

Frequently planted as a street tree and in gardens in southern Europe.

None.

Flowers and fruits; continuous in tropical climate.

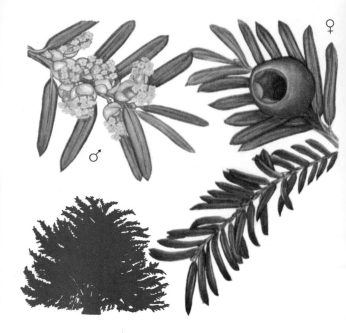

Fruit is a fleshy, oval berry, bright red in colour, about 1 cm long and containing one seed.

Eventually a medium-sized tree with a huge trunk. Leaves 1–3cm long, very dark green above, lighter green below and with a short stalk, arranged in 2 rows. Male flowers in cones. Seeds and leaves poisonous.

Woodlands and scrub on lime-rich soils in much of Europe; often planted as a hedge or in churchyards.

There are many cultivated varieties, differing mainly in their form and in the colour of their leaves, see page 125.

Flowering cones: March–April; fruits August–September.

Leaves soft, 2–2.5cm long, dark green above with 2 whitish bands below; spreading in 2 complex rows along each side of the branches.

A very tall conical tree. Leaf scars slightly prominent. Female cones drooping, green at first, brown when mature. 5–10cm long with prominent spiky, brown bracts. Cones shed whole.

Introduced and planted for timber in much of Europe.

Silver Fir p.98; Noble Fir p.99; (Western Hemlock p.121).

Flowering cones: March–April.

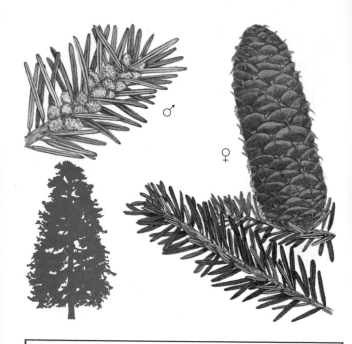

♂

♀

Leaves 1–2cm long, shining green above, silvery below, arranged in 4 rows along the branches when viewed from above.

A tall pyramidal tree. Leaves leave flat round scars on the twigs when they fall off. Female cones erect, in clusters near top of tree, green at first, mature cones brown, 10–14cm long, breaking up on tree to release seeds.

Forms mountain forests in central and southern Europe. Planted for timber throughout much of Europe.

Noble Fir p.99; (Spanish Fir p.121); Douglas Fir p.97.

Flowering cones: April.

NOBLE FIR

EVERGREEN, LARGE

Leaves 1.5–3.5cm long, leathery, strongly curved, blue-green on both sides; curving around the branches from below, in 4 rows.

A very tall conical tree. Leaves leave flat round scars on twigs when they fall off. Female cones erect, yellowish at first, purple-brown with green bracts when mature, up to 25cm long, breaking up on tree to release seeds.

Introduced and planted for timber in northern and western Europe; also for ornament in parks and gardens.

(Giant Fir p.121); Silver Fir p.98; Douglas Fir p.97.

Flowering cones: April–May.

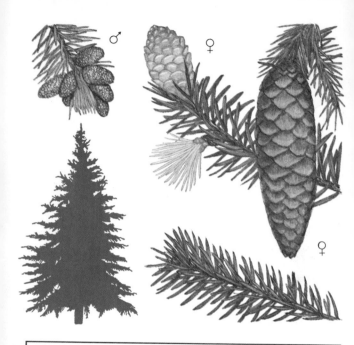

Leaves hard, green, 1–2cm long with pointed tips, spirally arranged on branches, not in rows.

A tall conical tree. Leaves leave peg-like projections on twigs when they fall off. Female cones erect and green at first, maturing brown and drooping, 10–15cm long, growing near the top of the tree, shed whole.

Upland areas in much of Europe; also planted in parks or for timber; young ones are used as Christmas trees.

Serbian Spruce p.101; (Sitka Spruce p.121); (Oriental Spruce p.121); (Blue Spruce p.121).

Flowering cones: May–June.

♀

♂

Leaves flattened, 1–2cm long with blunt tips, green above with 2 white bands below; spirally arranged on branches, not in rows.

A tall conical tree. Leaves leave peg-like projections on twigs when they fall off. Female cones drooping from topmost branches, red at first, maturing dark brown, 3-6cm long, shed whole.

Planted in northern Europe for timber; also in city parks and gardens since it is resistant to pollution.

Norway Spruce p.100; (Sitka Spruce p.121); (Oriental Spruce p.121); (Blue Spruce p.121).

Flowering cones: May.

Leaves 1–3cm long, growing in clusters of 30-40, very bright green especially in spring when new leaves appear.

A tall conical tree. Female cones have conspicuous red bracts when young, maturing into egg-shaped, brown cones, 2-3.5cm long, which remain on tree after the seeds are shed.

Planted for timber and in parks and gardens in much of Europe; often naturalized.

Japanese Larch p.103.

Flowering cones: March–April.

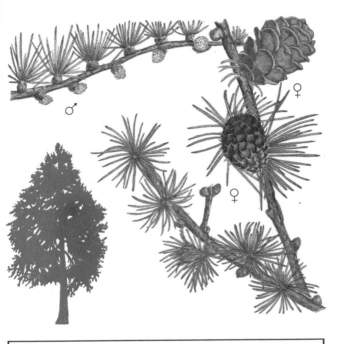

Leaves 1.5–3.5cm long, growing in clusters of about 40, bluish-green with two white bands on the lower surface.

A broad conical tree. Female cones have rather inconspicuous greenish bracts when young, maturing into rounded, egg-shaped, brown cones, 1.5–3.5cm long, remaining on the tree after the seeds are shed.

Planted for timber in northern and western areas of Europe.

European Larch p.102.

Flowering cones: March–April.

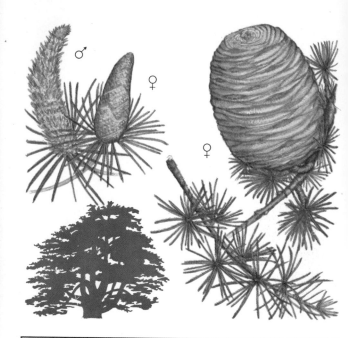

Leaves 2–3cm long, growing in clusters of 10–15, blue-green to dark green; young shoots grow horizontally.

A large tree with ascending branches forming a flat-topped, spreading crown. Male and female cones both large, upright and conspicuous, male cones grey-green, female cones brown, breaking up on tree to release seeds.

Pollution-tolerant species from the Middle East; widely planted in parks and churchyards.

Deodar Cedar p.105; (Atlas Cedar p.121).

Flowering cones: October–February.

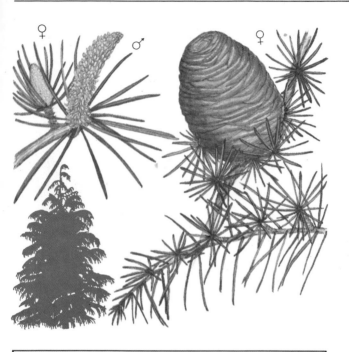

Leaves 2–5cm long, growing in clusters of 15–20, dark green or yellowish-green; young shoots arching downwards.

Young trees with weeping branches, mature trees broadly conical. Male and female cones both large, upright, conspicuous; male cones purple, female cones brown, breaking up on tree to release seeds.

Widely planted in parks and gardens throughout much of Europe and for timber in southern areas.

Cedar of Lebanon p.104; (Atlas Cedar p.121).

Flowering cones: November.

105

MARITIME PINE
EVERGREEN, MEDIUM

♂ ♀

Leaves 10–20cm long, growing in pairs, very thick and rigid, whitish-green, not particularly dense on the branches.

A medium-sized tree with widely spaced branches at the top. Mature female cones 8-22cm long, light shining brown, stalkless, remaining on tree after seeds are shed.

Light soils and dunes in the Mediterranean region; now grown in similar areas further north.

Scots Pine p.108; Austrian Pine p.107; (Monterey Pine p.121); (Stone Pine p.121).

Flowering cones: May–June.

AUSTRIAN PINE

EVERGREEN, LARGE

♂

♀

Leaves 10–15cm long, growing in pairs and very densely clothing the branches, very dark green, stiff, straight or twisted.

A tall tree with a crown of branches at the top. Mature female cones 5–8cm long, yellow-brown, almost stalkless, remaining on tree after seeds are shed.

Planted in shelter belts especially in coastal areas and on chalky soils in much of Europe.

Corsican Pine p.122); Scots Pine p.108; Maritime Pine p.106; (Aleppo Pine p.122).

Flowering cones: May–June.

107

♀

♂

Leaves 3–10cm long, blue-green and twisted, growing in pairs and sparsely clothing the branches.

A medium-sized to tall tree with a crown of branches at the top. Mature female cones 2–8cm long, grey-brown, on short stalks, remaining on tree after seeds are shed.

Most widely distributed of all the pines in Europe, growing on light sandy soils, especially in upland areas.

Austrian Pine p.107; Maritime Pine p.106; (Stone Pine p.121).

Flowering cones May–June.

AROLLA PINE
EVERGREEN, LARGE

♀

♂

Leaves 5–8cm long, stiff, dark green above and whitish below, growing in clusters of 5 and very densely clothing the branches.

A pyramidal tree with branches almost to the ground. Young shoots covered in distinctive orange-brown fur. Mature female cones purplish-brown, on short stalks, about 8cm long, shed whole.

Native to the Alps and Carpathian Mountains and also planted for timber in other areas of Europe.

(Bhutan Pine p.122); (Weymouth Pine p.122).

Flowering cones: May–June.

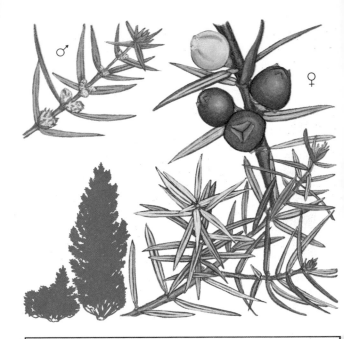

Fruit a green berry, changing to blue-black when ripening after a year on the plant, containing several seeds.

A spreading shrub or small tree. Leaves small, rigid and pointed, in whorls of 3, dark green below with a white stripe above. Male flowers in cones on separate trees from the female cones.

Chalk or limestone downlands and acid heathlands throughout Europe.

There are many cultivated varieties. (Prickly Juniper p.122); Chinese Juniper p.111.

Flowering cones: May–June; fruits September–October.

CHINESE JUNIPER
EVERGREEN, SMALL

Fruit a bluish-white berry, changing to purplish-brown when ripening after a year on the plant; containing several seeds.

A small conical tree. It has two kinds of leaves – juvenile, prickly, blue-green needles and adult, scale-like, dark green leaves closely pressed to the stems. Male and female flowering cones on separate trees.

Planted in parks, gardens and churchyards throughout much of Europe.

Common Juniper p.110; (Pencil Juniper p.122); (Phoenician Juniper p.122); ('Skyrocket' p.125).

Flowering cones: March–April; fruit takes 2 years to ripen.

Very distinctive appearance with thick, regularly arranged, horizontal or drooping branches clothed with large, thick, glossy green leaves.

A large, domed tree. Male and female cones on separate trees. Mature female cones round, brown, upright on upper sides of branches, breaking up on tree to release seeds. Male cones brown, in clusters, at tips of branches.

Introduced and planted in parks and gardens especially in western Europe.

None

Flowering cones: July.

112

Female cones numerous, conical in shape, about 1cm long, leathery, green at first, later brown; only middle three scales bear seeds, 2–3 on each scale.

A large pyramidal tree with an erect leading tip and feathery foliage which smells of pear-drops. Leaves opposite, green above, whitish beneath. Male cones minute, almost invisible on tips of shoots.

Introduced and widely planted for timber and as a hedge throughout Europe.

Lawson Cypress p.114; Leyland Cypress p.115; (White Cedar p.122); Common Cultivars p.125.

Flowering cones: March.

LAWSON CYPRESS
EVERGREEN, LARGE

♂

♀

Female cones numerous, round, about 8mm in diameter, green at first, later brown and woody with all 8 scales bearing seeds, 2–5 on each scale.

A large conical tree with a drooping leading tip and feathery foliage with a distinctive resinous scent. Leaves opposite, dark green above, whitish beneath. Male cones up to 5mm in diameter on tips of shoots.

Introduced and widely planted for timber and as a hedge throughout Europe.

There are many cultivated varieties, differing mainly in their size and shape, see page 125. Leyland Cypress p.115.

Flowering cones: February–April.

LEYLAND CYPRESS

EVERGREEN, LARGE

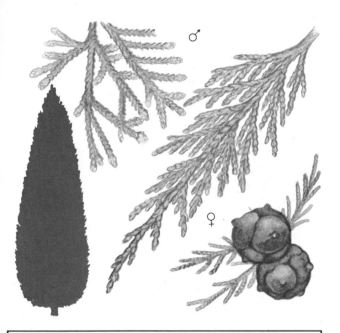

♂

♀

Male and female cones rare. Female cones, when produced, are round, brown and shiny, 2-3 cm in diameter with 4–8 scales, usually seedless.

A large conical tree with a leaning leading tip and feathery foliage with a resinous scent. Leaves opposite, green above, yellowish below.

Extensively planted as a hedging plant throughout much of Europe.

There are several cultivated varieties, differing mainly in the colour of their leaves, see page 125. Lawson Cypress p.114.

Flowering cones: March.

Female cones numerous, round and lumpy, about 3cm in diameter; green at first, later purple-brown and shiny; all 8 scales bear seeds, 8–20 on each scale.

A medium-sized domed tree with an erect leading tip and feathery, lemon-scented foliage. Leaves opposite, deep green. Male cones about 3mm in diameter on tips of shoots behind female cones.

Introduced and planted in southern and western Europe especially as a hedge plant.

There are several cultivated varieties, see p.125. Italian Cypress p.117; Leyland Cypress p.115.

Flowering cones: March.

116

This form of the Italian Cypress is a very narrow tree with ascending branches and ascending, feathery shoots with dark green, opposite leaves.

Female cones numerous, round, 2–4cm in diameter, green at first, later dull yellowish-grey, with 8–14 scales all bearing 8–20 seeds. Male cones about 4mm in diameter on tips of shoots.

Widely planted in Europe especially in the Mediterranean region where its upright form makes it conspicuous.

There is also a columnar form of this tree, p.122; (Monterey Cypress p.125).

Flowering cones: March.

Lookalikes & Cultivars

Almond Willow (1) A shrub. Leaves hairless, 3–8 times as long as broad. **Chinese Weeping Willow** (2) Long weeping branches have brown bark. **Peach** (3) Flowers deep pink; fruits velvety yellow-red peaches. **Rum Cherry** (4) A large tree. Leaves have orange hairs on undersides. **Japanese Spindle Tree** (5) A small evergreen tree most often found in south Europe. **Sour Cherry** (6) A shrub with red cherries – the Morello cherry. **Grey Willow** (7) A shrub with slender catkins and narrow leaves. **Black Poplar** (8) A large tree with black bark and bosses on trunk. **Black Italian Poplar** (9) A large tree with black bark but no bosses. **Japonica** (10) Flowers scarlet in small clusters on old wood.

White Mulberry (1) Leaves shiny, food for silkworms. Fruit white or pink. **Green Alder** (2) Leaves with pronounced double teeth and pointed tips. **Grey Alder** (3) Leaves like those of Green Alder, but grey beneath. **Dutch Elm** (4) A large domed tree with many suckers. **Eastern Strawberry Tree** (5) A Mediterranean tree. Bark reddish-brown, peeling. **Rhododendron** (6) Flowers large, lilac-purple, in dense clusters. **Citron** (7) Large yellow fruit with thick rind. **Seville Orange** (8) Fruit with sour flesh and thick rough orange rind. **Copper Beech** (9) Leaves distinctive – coppery purple in colour.

119

Lookalikes & Cultivars

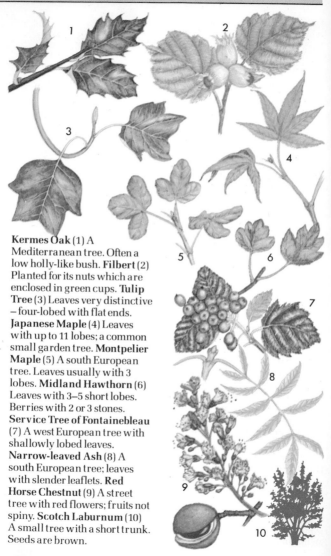

Kermes Oak (1) A Mediterranean tree. Often a low holly-like bush. **Filbert** (2) Planted for its nuts which are enclosed in green cups. **Tulip Tree** (3) Leaves very distinctive – four-lobed with flat ends. **Japanese Maple** (4) Leaves with up to 11 lobes; a common small garden tree. **Montpelier Maple** (5) A south European tree. Leaves usually with 3 lobes. **Midland Hawthorn** (6) Leaves with 3–5 short lobes. Berries with 2 or 3 stones. **Service Tree of Fontainebleau** (7) A west European tree with shallowly lobed leaves. **Narrow-leaved Ash** (8) A south European tree; leaves with slender leaflets. **Red Horse Chestnut** (9) A street tree with red flowers; fruits not spiny. **Scotch Laburnum** (10) A small tree with a short trunk. Seeds are brown.

Lookalikes & Cultivars

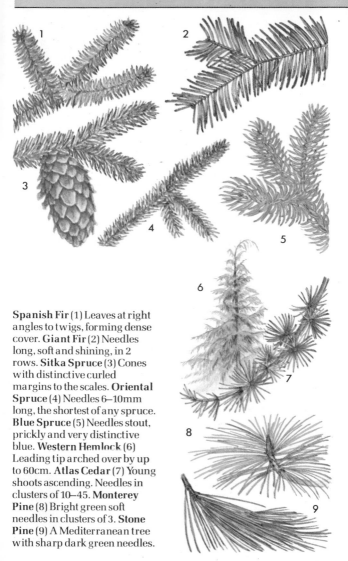

Spanish Fir (1) Leaves at right angles to twigs, forming dense cover. **Giant Fir** (2) Needles long, soft and shining, in 2 rows. **Sitka Spruce** (3) Cones with distinctive curled margins to the scales. **Oriental Spruce** (4) Needles 6–10mm long, the shortest of any spruce. **Blue Spruce** (5) Needles stout, prickly and very distinctive blue. **Western Hemlock** (6) Leading tip arched over by up to 60cm. **Atlas Cedar** (7) Young shoots ascending. Needles in clusters of 10–45. **Monterey Pine** (8) Bright green soft needles in clusters of 3. **Stone Pine** (9) A Mediterranean tree with sharp dark green needles.

Lookalikes & Cultivars

Corsican Pine (1) A small tree with many level, regular branches. **Aleppo Pine** (2) A Mediterranean tree with pale grey bark on twigs. **Bhutan Pine** (3) Clusters of 5 very long, soft, slim needles. **Weymouth Pine** (4) Clusters of 5 short horizontal blue-green needles. **Prickly Juniper** (5) A shrub with prickly needles having 2 white stripes. **Pencil Juniper** (6) A tall slender juniper. **Phoenician Juniper** (7) A Mediterranean tree or shrub with scaly branches. **White Cedar** (8) Foliage yellow-green in vertical twisted sprays. **Italian Cypress** (9) A broad columnar tree.

122

Lookalikes & Cultivars

Japanese Cherries(1–7)
'Amanogawa' (1) Branches ascending to form a very narrow tree. '**Shimidsu Sakura**' (2) Wide spreading branches form a flattened crown. '**Tai-Haku**' (3) Branches spreading. Flowers single, white. '**Hokusai**' (4) One of the earliest to flower. A wide-spreading tree.
'**Shirotae**' (5) A small tree with drooping branches. '**Ukon**' (6) A spreading tree with green-tinged flowers. **Cheal's Weeping Cherry** (7) Branches may touch the ground.
Magnolias
M. grandiflora (8) An evergreen tree with large leathery leaves. **M. stellata** (9) A small tree. Flowers have many narrow petals. **M. campbelli** (10) A large tree with deep pink flowers.

Lookalikes & Cultivars

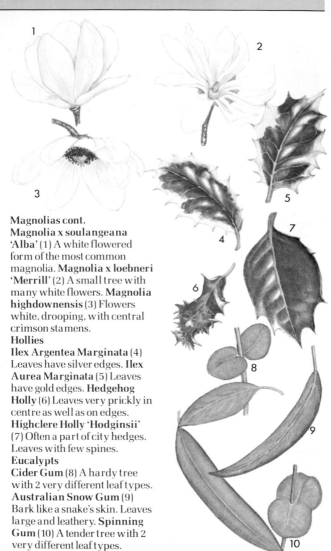

Magnolias cont.
**Magnolia x soulangeana
'Alba'** (1) A white flowered
form of the most common
magnolia. **Magnolia x loebneri
'Merrill'** (2) A small tree with
many white flowers. **Magnolia
highdownensis** (3) Flowers
white, drooping, with central
crimson stamens.
Hollies
Ilex Argentea Marginata (4)
Leaves have silver edges. **Ilex
Aurea Marginata** (5) Leaves
have gold edges. **Hedgehog
Holly** (6) Leaves very prickly in
centre as well as on edges.
Highclere Holly 'Hodginsii'
(7) Often a part of city hedges.
Leaves with few spines.
Eucalypts
Cider Gum (8) A hardy tree
with 2 very different leaf types.
Australian Snow Gum (9)
Bark like a snake's skin. Leaves
large and leathery. **Spinning
Gum** (10) A tender tree with 2
very different leaf types.

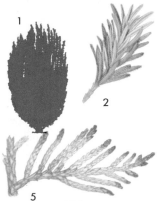

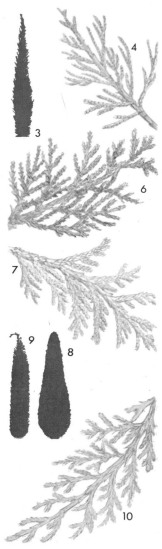

Upright Yew (1) A narrow upright tree with very dark green foliage. **Upright Yellow Yew** (2) A narrow upright tree with yellow foliage. **Pencil Juniper 'Skyrocket'** (3) An extremely narrow tree; eventually a tall one. **Monterey Cypress 'Donard Gold'** (4) A conical tree with golden-yellow foliage. **Western Red Cedar 'Zebrina'** (5) A conical tree with green and yellow banded foliage. **Lawson Cypress 'Pembury Blue'** (6) A conical tree with blue foliage. **Lawson Cypress 'Stewartii'** (7) A conical tree with yellow foliage. **Lawson Cypress 'Pottenii'** (8) A dense conical tree with deep green foliage. **Lawson Cypress 'Columnaris'** (9) A dense narrow columnar tree with grey-green foliage. **Leyland Cypress 'Castlewellan Gold'** (10) A columnar hedging tree with yellow foliage.

Index and Check-list

Keep a record of your sightings by inserting a tick in the box.

Glossary of Terms

Axil The more-or-less V-shaped angle made by the junc
between a leaf and a stem or twig.
Boss A rough area on a trunk where many shoots grow.
Bract A green leafy structure which has a flower in its axil,
which may remain on the plant with the fruit. Bracts v
enormously in size, shape and function.
Capsule A dry fruit which splits open to release the seeds.
Catkin A drooping spike of small flowers. Male catkins proc
the pollen; the female catkins are pollinated and then develop
fruiting catkins which bear the seeds.
Cone The flowers and fruit of a conifer – a cone-bearing tree. M
cones produce pollen; female cones produce the seeds. The ma
brownish, woody seed-bearing cones are the most conspicu
and may be large and conical or small and conical.
Deciduous A deciduous tree is one which loses its leave
winter.
Evergreen An evergreen tree is one which bears leaves thro
out the year.
Fruits These contain the seeds. They may be dry or juicy, brow
brightly coloured, prickly or smooth etc.
Garden escape A cultivated garden plant which is growing i
wild.
Hybrid A plant which has originated from crossing one speci
plant with another. Hybrids may be man-made or natural and
show characteristics of both parents. They are always design
by a 'x' in the Latin name.
Opposite leaves Leaves growing in pairs on opposite sides
stem or twig. This condition is relatively uncommon v
compared to the condition known as 'alternate leaves' in whicl
leaves grow alternately from each side of the twig.
Pollarded A tree is said to be pollarded when it has been c
the ground several times and has then developed several trur
Shelter belt A belt of shrubs or trees planted to form a v
break.
Shoot A new young growth.
Stamens The pollen producing structures of a flower.
Sucker A shoot growing directly from the roots of a tree or sh
it may be growing some distance from the parent plant and
eventually form a new tree.
Terminal Borne at the end of a stem or twig.